COMMUNION

TRUTH
VS.
TRADITION

McDougal & Associates
Servants of Christ and Stewards of the
Mysteries of God

COMMUNION

TRUTH
VS.
TRADITION

BY

JERRY FITCH

Published by:

McDougal & Associates
18896 Greenwell Springs Road
Greenwell Springs, LA 70739

www.ThePublishedWord.com

McDougal & Associates is an organization dedicated to
spreading the Gospel of the Lord Jesus Christ to as many
people as possible in the shortest time possible.

ISBN: 978-1-950398-05-8

Printed in the U.S., the U.K. and Australia
For Worldwide Distribution

DEDICATION

This book is especially dedicated to the ones I love the most:

To my wife and faithful companion in the ministry, Monique. Without your faith and faithful support, this book would not have been possible.

To my three living children—Jerry Jr., Julie (Our Flower) and Justin. You are the best children I could have ever dreamed of.

To the memory of my father, Wesley Fitch, my son Jared (Bubba), and my brother Wesley. Rest in peace.

ACKNOWLEDGEMENTS

It is with deep feelings of pain and, yet, great relief that I dedicate this book to the many who have been negatively affected by the lack of understanding that has come forth from our churches across the land concerning Communion, its purpose and its benefits.

As you will read in the following pages, the Communion we know today is of Western thought and practice. Because we are not of the country that originated the concepts of Communion, we often do not follow the same rules. Does our failure to live up to Western standards make us less accepted or less part of the family? Can I call you Brother or Sister? Am I even a member of the same family? Do I love Jesus less than others? Am I somehow less worthy than they? Do not I hold the same office, place and posture?

In the penning of this book, I have remembered the times I personally was not allowed to receive Communion because of my status. I was not accepted by others. We must each ask ourselves, "How would that make you feel?"

I remembered taking over the pastorate of a church in West Monroe, Louisiana, where the husband of one of the young church ladies had not been allowed to receive Communion because he was not considered "good enough." Yes, that happens right here in America! That bothered me, and I knew it bothered God.

The first chance I got, I ministered on the subject of Communion and then opened the Communion to anyone who wanted to participate, and that man did. What a liberty and release he sensed that day. It was the first time in his long Christian experience that he had been "allowed" to receive the body and blood of Jesus through Communion, and it totally liberated him. He was also set free that day from man's lack of understanding and brought into a God awareness that revolutionized his life. I knew exactly how he felt because that was how I felt when I was finally able to enjoy the blessings of Communion.

So, to those who have felt left out, unappreciated, condemned and ostracized and have been made to feel unworthy, I dedicate this book. I dedicate it to your wounds, in expectation that healing will arise in you through Communion, as God intended.

There is so much to receive and discern in the act of Communion. This small writing is not all-inclusive, but it can be the beginning of a journey of a lifetime with the Jesus you have received as Lord and Savior.

Together,
Dr. Jerry Fitch

CONTENTS

For as often as ye eat this bread, and drink this cup, ye do shew the Lord's death till he come. Wherefore whosoever shall eat this bread, and drink this cup of the Lord, unworthily, shall be guilty of the body and blood of the Lord. But let a man examine himself, and so let him eat of that bread, and drink of that cup. For he that eateth and drinketh unworthily, eateth and drinketh damnation to himself, not discerning the Lord's body. For this cause many are weak and sickly among you, and many sleep.

1 Corinthians 11:26-30

FOREWORD BY
GERALD DOGGETT

The Bible records:

*Wisdom is the principal thing; therefore get
wisdom: and with all thy getting get understanding.* Proverbs 4:7

While millions of dollars are spent on health
clubs, jogging clothes, diets and other types
of physical fitness activities, to get the body
into shape, our minds and spirits are starving.
As Christians, we must be very careful not to
adopt a Pharisee mentality, keeping the outside
beautiful at the exclusion of the inner man.

The following pages will prompt your
thinking regarding an ordinance of the

church that is often taken as sheer ritualism. May God forgive us. Give serious thought as my close personal friend, Jerry Fitch, shares his heart concerning this matter of Christian Communion.

Jerry brings his wisdom and understanding to you backed by a personal devotional life that has birthed many powerful messages. His insights will challenge your mind and spirit to a greater understanding of this most misunderstood sacrament.

After finishing this book, I believe your future participation in the communion service will offer a much greater meaning to your heart and life.

Gerald Doggett

INTRODUCTION

The Holy Spirit spoke to my heart one day during a council meeting I attended. He said, "To minister the Word is your calling, to enhance that ministry is your responsibility, to neglect to do so is your loss." From that moment on, I determined to diligently search out the truths of God with more fervor than ever before. Studying God's Word had been a part of my life for a long time; now it *was* my life.

In this book, I am not trying to establish some theological treatise for the Church. Neither do I intend to create some new doctrine. My only purpose in writing this is to expose the errors of tradition that have hindered the Church from moving in the fullness of God.

This writing is not in any way conclusive on the matter of communion, and it is not meant to be. I pray, however, that it will give you new keys to unlock the door to the answers that hungry people everywhere are searching for.

To some, what you read here may cause anger to stir in your heart. To others, it will minister life and liberty. With both responses, I am pleased, for this will lead you to study more of the truths of God and make any necessary adjustment to your thinking. Change hurts, but do as the Spirit spoke to my heart, "Improve that which is good and change that which is not."

Jerry Fitch

1

A PRELUDE TO PASSOVER

Philip saith unto him, Lord, show us the Father, and it sufficeth us.   John 14:8

And there were certain Greeks among them that came up to worship at the feast: the same came therefore to Philip, which was of Bethsaida of Galilee, and desired him, saying, Sir, we would see Jesus.   John 12:20-21

Philip said, *"Show us the Father."* The Greeks said, *"We would see Jesus."* I am fully persuaded that if we would show the world Jesus Christ, they would come to see Him as He really is. The world is tired of our programs, our religious ceremonies and our sanctimonious attitudes. They would see Jesus!

The world is tired of our programs,
our religious ceremonies
and our sanctimonious attitudes.
They would see Jesus!

A Prelude to Passover

False concepts derived by our private inter-pretation of God's Word have only shown the world the fallibility of our understanding. Like Philip, they cry, "Show us the Father!" Well, in Communion, you can see the Father, but our traditions have discouraged many.

During the week of Passover, Jesus shared many lasting truths with His disciples. If we can know and understand these truths today, they can help us understand His work and His will for our individual lives. What preceded the Passover prepared His followers for the Passover and also for all what followed.

There were three towns that Jesus visited that week, sharing important truths with His friends. Let's see if understanding them can help us today in the twenty-first century.

The first visit is recorded in John 11:54. There is says that Jesus visited a town called Ephraim *"near to the wilderness."* Angry Jews were even then seeking to do Him harm, but, as John recorded earlier, His hour had *"not yet come"* (John 7:30). On previous occasions, these people had sought to kill Jesus, but He had escaped, for His hour had not yet come (see John 8:59). Even early in His ministry, zealous Jewish men had sought to kill Him by casting Him off of a hill near Nazareth (see Luke 4:28-30), but He, *"passing through the midst of them went his way"* (verse 30). His hour had not yet come.

On another occasion, recorded in John 10:31, angry men were intent upon stoning Jesus, but, again. He escaped out of their hands (see verse 39), for His hour had not yet come.

In Kingdom understanding, it is important that we realize the fact that God has called us to do a work. He has a plan and a purpose for our lives, and there is no devil or human who can stop that plan. Psalm 37:23 states this truth so beautifully:

> *The steps of a good man are ordered by the Lord: and he delighteth in his way.*

The second reason for Jesus' stop at Ephraim was that He wanted to continue to prepare the disciples for the final events of His life.

God has called us to do a work.
He has a plan and a purpose
for our lives,
and there is no devil or person
who can stop that plan!

I believe this was a time of spiritual renewal for them.

In Jerusalem, the confusion and the frenzy of Jesus' enemies were at an all-time high, even to the point that if anyone knew the whereabouts of Jesus, they were to report it or face judgment (see John 11:57). But in Ephraim, all was peaceful and undisturbed, and the disciples were safe with the Prince of Peace! He who calmed the storms was giving them peace and assurance in the midst of the current storm, and, at the same time, He was preparing them for the greatest storm of their lives, as well as the greatest storm of *His* own life.

Oh, my friend, come aside to Ephraim for spiritual renewal. Come and gain strength at the feet of Jesus. All week long you are submitted to fears, doubts and confusion, but come aside to Jesus, and He will renew your strength. There is a place in God where you can escape for spiritual renewal.

Then, six days before the Passover, Jesus entered Bethany (see John 12). Bethany, as you will recall, was the home of Mary, Martha and Lazarus. In that town, therefore, there was much dissension concerning Jesus. It was in Bethany where deep cried unto deep, and Lazarus was raised from the dead. An added revelation dealing with prayer and the raising of Lazarus is appropriate here.

When Jesus received the report of the condition of Lazarus, He sent a message to Mary and Martha that Lazarus' sickness was *"not unto death, but for the glory of God, that the Son of God might be glorified thereby"* (John 11:4). Can you see how the raising of Lazarus from the dead *before* the Passover would prepare the disciples for the truths to be shared *during* Passover?

John 11 is often used during funerals, but let us examine it more in its context and reap benefits that are not only applicable for the future, but also for the present.

Lazarus is dead.   John 11:14

This was the stark reality that Jesus had spoken to His disciples before they set off for

Can you see how the raising of Lazarus from the dead <u>before</u> the Passover would prepare the disciples for the truths to be shared <u>during</u> Passover?

A Prelude to Passover

Bethany. When it was rumored that He was nearby, Martha left the house and went to meet Him. When she did this, she was breaking Jewish custom. An earlier lesson had taught her that, when it came to Jesus, He superseded the Law.

Martha told Jesus that if He had been there, Lazarus would not have died. She added:

> *But I know, that even now, whatsoever thou wilt ask of God, God will give it thee.*   John 11:22

Jesus told Martha that Lazarus would live again, and this is where we get the popular funeral messages. But that was not all that Jesus had in mind. Martha answered with this declaration:

> *I know that he shall rise again in the resurrection at the last day.*   John 11:24

But Jesus answered her:

> *I am the resurrection, and the life: he* [Lazarus] *that believeth in me, though he* [Lazarus] *were dead, yet shall he* [Lazarus] *live.* John 11:25

Jesus was not planning a funeral message; He was preparing a resurrection message! And not only for Lazarus, but also for Himself. (I will elaborate more on this in Chapter 3.)

In the next scene, Jesus was at the burial ground. John 11:33 shows us a model for prayer that He gave to all of God's people that day. It says:

> *He* [Jesus] *groaned in the spirit, and was troubled.*

Twice in the scriptures it is stated that Jesus groaned within Himself or in the Spirit. Romans 8:26 gives to us a clear example for prayer:

> *Likewise the Spirit also helpeth our infirmities* [our inability to produce the needed results]: *for we know not what we should pray for as we ought: but the Spirit itself maketh intercession for us with groanings which cannot be uttered.*

Although the words *groanings* and *groaned* are two separate words in the Greek, both tend to

Although the words
<u>groanings</u> and <u>groaned</u>
are two separate words
in the Greek,
both tend to lead
to the same principle,
that of being moved to action!

lead to the same principle, that of being moved to action.

Jesus then prayed:

> *Father, I thank thee that thou hast heard me. And I knew that thou hearest me always: but because of the people which stand by I said it, that they may believe that thou hast sent me.* John 11:41-42

When was it that God first heard Jesus praying? And when exactly had Jesus prayed? The people standing by obviously had not heard Him pray, yet He said to His Father, "I said it so that the people around Me might believe that You sent Me." I submit to you that it was during the time Jesus *"groaned in the Spirit"* that intercession was made according to the will of God, and it was in that moment that Father God heard Jesus' prayer. Afterward, Jesus glorified the Father before the people and allowed them to know that the Father had heard Him, so that they might believe.

A Prelude to Passover

The next words out of Jesus' mouth were these, and He spoke them in a very loud voice:

Lazarus come forth.   John 11:43

What happened when He said that?

He that was dead came forth.
                              John 11:44

This setting, that preceded Jesus' final entry into Bethany in John 12, prepares us to receive the next truth upon His return. Simply stated, those whom Jesus has ministered to in a special way (supernaturally) are now to minister to Him. Once God has ministered to you, then it is your turn to minister to Him.

Now Mary took some very costly ointment and anointed the feet of Jesus, and, in doing so, manifested the ultimate expression of love. She gave Him her best. Instead of Jesus serving her, she now became a servant to Him. Also

Once God has ministered to you, then it is your turn to minister to Him!

note that ministry leads others to believe (see John 12:9-11).

The very next day Jesus entered the third city prior to the Passover, and this was the Holy City itself, Jerusalem. What was His purpose in going where He was hated and His life was in danger? He wanted people to recognize Him as King (see John 12:12-19). Earlier, He had not allowed it (see John 6:14-15). Now He declared it.

This entry of Jesus into the Holy City is commonly called the Triumphal Entry, and it included what He expected of His disciples and His Church. He now establishes:

1. The purpose of the church (see Matthew 21:13). His church is to be a *"house of prayer."*
2. The plan of God (see Matthew 21:14 and Matthew 6:9). *"Thy will be done."*
3. The praise of His name (see Matthew 21:15-16). *"Have ye never read?"*
4. Faith in Him and in Father God (see Matthew 21:21-22). *"If ye have faith." "And*

all things, whatsoever ye shall ask in prayer, believing, ye shall receive."

The week of the Passover, Jesus showed us that He is able to bring comfort and peace where there is none. There is spiritual renewal for the one who will come aside and seek Him. Next He ministered concerning the importance of what we do after we have been ministered to (we are then to minister). And, finally, He shared with His friends that God has a purpose for the Church.

Allow the heart of Jesus that is exemplified in these visitations to be part of the understanding that you receive in Communion. These truths will not only enlighten you, but will also brighten your participation in the Communion as you receive it with a glorious expectation.

The week of the Passover,
Jesus showed us that He is
able to bring comfort and
peace where there is none!

2

COMMUNION: MEANS AND OPPORTUNITY

And thus shall ye eat it; with your loins girded, your shoes on your feet, and your staff in your hand; and ye shall eat it in haste: it is the LORD's passover. Exodus 12:11

The first Passover is recorded in Exodus 12. God lost no time in making the Israelites to know Who the Passover was for (*"It is the LORD's passover)"* and its purpose (*"And this day shall be unto you for a memorial,"* verse 14). This was not just for that one event. It was for all time to come—*"Ye shall keep it a feast to the Lord throughout your generations"* (same verse). Through Passover, all genera-

Through Passover,
all generations were to understand
the omnipotence of God!

tions were to understand the omnipotence of God.

The setting for the Passover seems to indicate a number of truths that are largely overlooked in Christianity today. First of all, Israel was not a free nation at the time. The Israelites were in bondage to the Egyptians, and the reason for the Passover was to deliver them from that bondage.

I am sorry to say that Christianity, for a number of years now, has advocated teachings concerning Communion that are not necessarily biblical. For instance, we have been taught that if we partake of Communion *"unworthily"* (a term usually defined as meaning "being in sin"), we are in danger of damnation. This teaching is taken out of context from the writings of Paul in 1 Corinthians 11:27.

This teaching has caused horrors that have been passed down through generations, limiting participation in this holy ordinance of the Church to only a select few. It is the deliberate intention of this author to destroy the empty theological notions that have robbed many of the greatest benefits available to mankind through participation in the Communion. This misconception has sometimes denied the privilege of Communion to the average Christian. Maybe Christians are like they are because they have been filled with fear through false doctrines.

The particular false teaching I refer to states: "If there is sin in your life, then you'd better not take Communion." Is that true? Let's examine the Passover, upon which Communion is based, and see if that statement holds true.

First, as previously mentioned, the Israelites were in bondage at the time of the Passover. Secondly, they were in a land that was not their own and not the land God had promised them. After many years in this oppressive situation, they began to cry out to Him.

Now, if the Passover is to be applied spiritually to our lives, and it has those three conditions prevalent, then the truth is that Communion serves as a means and is not an exception. Here are some important points to remember:

The Israelites were in bondage at the time of the Passover. They were in a land that was not their own and not the land God had promised them. After many years in this oppressive situation, they began to cry out to Him!

1. The Passover meant salvation to the Israelites. Exodus 12:13 states, *"When I see the blood, I will pass over you."* This emphatically speaks of salvation. How did that salvation come? In the preparation for the Passover, blood was shed, and that blood was then applied to the houses of the Israelites. This was not for a people who were without sin. It was not the people who were *"without blemish."* It was the lamb that was *"without blemish"* (Exodus 12:5). Therefore, Communion serves as a means of obtaining forgiveness. God said, *"I will pass over you."*

   How many souls have been turned away from the family of God because they had to "clean up" before they could participate in Communion? What a tragedy! The best opportunity to win souls to the Kingdom of God is through Communion, and yet we close the door on this means because of ignorance of His Word.

2. Communion serves as a means of deliverance from bondage and, ultimately, inheriting the

land God has promised. Exodus 12:25-27 states that God smote the enemies of Israel and that they would ultimately *"come to the land which the LORD will give* [them] *according as he hath promised"* (verse 25). Communion, then, serves as a means to destroy the enemy's work in people's lives and sets them on the path to receiving the Kingdom of God.

In Exodus 12:12, God said, *"I will pass through the land of Egypt this night,"* and He spoke this of judgment. But that judgment was not to be upon the people of Israel. It was to be upon their enemies!

If a person receiving Communion is not in right standing with God, and that would signify death to them, then we would all be dead. Rest assured, none of us are perfect yet. But God is not trying to destroy the individual. He is wanting to destroy what is destroying the individual. He loves the sinner; it is the sin He hates.

Once a man or woman has allowed God to begin to work in their life, then they can proceed to walk and live in the dimension

If a person receiving Communion
is not in right standing with God,
and that would signify death to
them, then we would all be dead!

of the Kingdom. With the realized truth that God is working to destroy things in his life that do not pertain to godliness, then he or she can proceed to establish the Kingdom of God: *"When ye come to the land which the* LORD *will give you."*

3. Communion serves as a means for healing and health to the participant. There is a divine protection ministered in Communion: *"the plague shall not be upon you"* (Exodus 12:13). Any radical who advocates plagues (sicknesses) as a blessing from God to His people should read this. As you dwell in covenant relationship with God (and, by the way, Communion is a covenant (see Chapter 4): *"neither shall any plague come nigh thy dwelling"* (Psalm 91:10).

Communion also serves as an agent in healing. Speculation dictates the impossibility of two to three million people being together and not even one of them being sick. On that first Passover night, God performed a mass healing.

The word *healeth,* as used in Exodus 15:26, indicates that there were sick people, possibly even some halt, maimed and crippled. When God said, *"I am the Lord that healeth thee,"* He was implying that they *were* sick, but He healed them.

The Hebrew word translated *healeth* is *rapha,* which is interpreted as "to mend, to cure, to heal, to repair, to make whole." You don't mend something that is not torn. You don't repair something that is not broken. You don't cure something that is not sick. And you don't make whole something that is already perfect. God manifested a Kingdom truth the night of the Passover when He healed the Israelites of their infirmities, and there was not one feeble one among their tribes.

So, why refrain from God's best, when He has offered to you health and healing in Communion? My friend, the greatest means awaits you as you participate in Communion. The world will begin to unfold and you can enter in with a dimension of Kingdom understand-

When God said, "I am the Lᴏʀᴅ that healeth thee," He was implying that they were sick, but He healed them!

ing that will enable you to accomplish the task before you.

Now that we have looked at the importance of Communion through the means it provides, let us examine the opportunities available for the participant:

1. Communion is an opportunity for fellowship. Matthew 26:20 states that at the time of the Passover Jesus *"sat down with the twelve."* Although Jesus was about to be offered up in death, He made time to fellowship with His chosen ones. Communion served them as an opportunity to fellowship with Jesus. It seems that one of God's desires is to fellowship with His people. He sought fellowship with Adam and Eve, His crowning creation, in the *"cool of the day"* (Genesis 3:8). Jesus prayed, *"Father, I will that they also, whom thou hast given me, be with me where I am"* (John 17:24). Then, before He left to go back to the Father, He said to His disciples, *"Lo, I am with you always, even unto the end of the*

world" (Matthew 28:20). And the list goes on.

All of this describes the longing of God to fellowship with His creation. But hear me, the opportunity for fellowship is also man to God, for embedded in the spirit of man is the desire to know his beginnings. Jesus offers us an opportunity for spiritual fulfillment in fellowship through Communion.

2. Communion serves as an opportunity for self-examination. Matthew 26:22 records the question of the disciple of Jesus, *"Lord, is it I?"* The closer to the light you get, the more your heart is revealed. *"Is it I?"* I can only imagine the depths of what God is trying to say to us today. He is the personification of perfection, God manifest in the flesh, and yet He is ready to fellowship with you and me and allow us to examine our own personal lives in the light that only He can shed. This gives us the opportunity to see ourselves in relationship to Him. And the light that reveals sin is the same light that dispels the

Communion serves as an
opportunity for self-examination!

darkness it shines upon. This brings me to
the next point.

3. Communion is an opportunity for reconciliation. Through Communion, a wayward
one is entreated to return to fellowship with
God. The diligent search of the disciples for
who it was who would betray Christ opened
the way for Him to invite Judas to reconsider
what he was about to do. Here was a man
who had already sinned in his heart, and yet
Jesus invited him to participate in Communion. Think about that!

Judas was now invited to dip his bread in the
sop (see John 13:26). What was the sop? It
was apparently just bread that was dipped
in a special sauce prepared for the feast.
The important thing to see here is that the
custom in the east was that the host would
give a "sop" to a guest he desired to honor
in a special way. In this way, Jesus showed
His love to the man who was about to betray Him. Apart from the honor, this could
also be interpreted as an appeal to Judas to

be reconciled back to God and changed his ways.

If there were no other proof, this one act of Communion should totally dispel the theology that a sinner is not to participate in Communion. If he would participate in Communion as he should, with an open heart to receive all that God has, he just might possibly no longer be a sinner. Thank God for His love that overrules our false assumptions and provides a way for reconciliation through Communion.

With proper understanding, the sinner is to be led to salvation through Communion. That is what God intended. The Israelites partook of the Passover and, through it, God implemented their salvation, deliverance, healing and inheritance. And then He led them out of bondage.

Let us not be so dogmatic in our theological interpretation of the scriptures that it dilutes the loving intent of God for humanity. Communion is one of God's ways of interacting

If a sinner would participate in Communion as he should, with an open heart to receive all that God has, he just might possibly no longer be a sinner!

with mankind. Do not allow your piety to interfere with the program of God to reconcile a lost world unto Himself.

3

COMMUNION: PAST AND PRESENT

Now the first day of the feast of unleavened bread the disciples came to Jesus, saying unto him, Where wilt thou that we prepare for thee to eat the passover?

And he said, Go into the city to such a man, and say unto him, The Master saith, My time is at hand; I will keep the passover at thy house with my disciples.

And the disciples did as Jesus had appointed them; and they made ready the passover.

Matthew 26:17-19

Many areas of God's Word strike an un-matched and unmatchable interest in my mind. Little things in it seems to lure me into a search for the depth of their meaning. Such is the subject of the Passover. A deep desire to understand Communion has caused me to seek out the truths that are deeper than what can be expressed in mere words. That desire to search the deep is the reason this book is being written.

You can go to a local bookstore or search online and find seemingly endless numbers of volumes on subjects such as faith, love, healing, church administration and church growth and countless commentaries, illustrators, word studies and biblical studies. But, try as you will, there are very few books to be found written concerning Communion. I believe this is either because we have accepted the "norm" that has been handed down through generations and feel that nothing more needs to be said, or perhaps, it is because authors fear to tread on territories of revelation that may cause others to take a stand against them. Whatever the case, I stand eternally grateful for the revelation of God to my heart concerning Communion.

A deep desire to understand Communion has caused me to seek out the truths that are deeper than what can be expressed in mere words!

I know that some will refute parts of what I have written here, but struggle as they will, God honors His Word. These revelations have not only come supernaturally to my heart, but as I have ministered them, God has honored His Word.

Matthew 26 takes us back to the night of the last Passover Jesus celebrated with His disciples. My personal attention seems to always focus on the verses that say:

> *And as they were eating, Jesus took bread, and blessed it, and brake it, and gave it to the disciples, and said, Take, eat; this is my body. And he took the cup, and gave thanks, and gave it to them, saying, Drink ye all of it; for this is my blood of the new testament, which is shed for many for the remission of sins.*
> Matthew 26:26-28

I have often wondered: what is *the blessing* and *the thanks* that Jesus pronounced upon the Passover meal? I, like the rest of the Christians who traditionally partake of Communion, have heard *"blessings"* pronounced over the bread and the drink, but too often these blessings seemed to be just good words that lacked true meaning. Personally, I have never been comfortable with taking Communion as a mere ritual, and I have often found the prayers offered to be empty and without depth of meaning, and this is in direct contrast to what God intended for Communion.

When we say our little prayers and move on, we miss out on the blessings of the Kingdom, and all because of a lack of understanding of everything pertaining to that Communion meal. We have overlooked aspects of Communion for which we have no answer.

For years, I searched commentaries for the answers, to appease my spiritual appetite, only to come up empty. Then one day it struck me: my former employer and friend was a devout Jew. Year after year, he would leave home and join other Jews to celebrate Passover. Surely he would know more of the true meaning.

I was rather embarrassed to ask this man about a subject I, as a pastor, was expected to be familiar

When we say our little prayers and move on, we miss out on the blessings of the Kingdom, and all because of a lack of understanding of everything pertaining to that Communion meal!

with. But my desire to know more about Communion outweighed my embarrassment and caused me to pick up the phone and call him.

When I asked him about the Passover blessing, I was not disappointed. Word for word, and without hesitation, he quoted to me, first, the Hebrew prayer prayed at Passover, and then he gave me the English translation of it.

The moment I heard this prayer, my spirit was overwhelmed, and I took a moment to rejoice. My hunger was finally appeased, my understanding enlightened, and I felt assured that the Kingdom of God could now be expressed in this matter.

Remember that Jesus took bread and blessed it and then did the same with wine. The custom was that the head of the household would be the one to pronounce this universal blessing over the elements of the Passover meal. The exact prayer over the bread in Hebrew is this:

Baruh Atah Adonai Eloheinu Meleh ha-olam asher kidshanu b'mitzvo-tav v'tzivanu al ahilat matzah.

In English, the prayer says:

We praise You, O Lord our God, King of the Universe, Who brings forth bread from the earth.

The next thing Jesus said was, "*Take, eat; this is my body.*" The connection is this: the disciples were, right then, concerned over the threats upon Jesus' life. Jesus was saying to them, "My hour is come, but don't worry. God is taking His Bread from the earth."

Seventeen times in the Gospels Jesus is referred to as *"the bread of life"* (for instance, John 6:35). Jesus was advising His disciples that He would be killed and then buried but that God the Father would take the Bread, Jesus, through the resurrection, from the earth. Thus, in the blessing of the bread, Jesus foretold His resurrection. And, because He lives, we can live also!

For centuries the Jewish people had prayed this prayer, but this time One identified Himself as the Bread they were to partake of: *"This is MY body!"*

For centuries the Jewish people had prayed this prayer, but this time One identified Himself as the Bread they were to partake of: "This is MY body!"

Next, Jesus took the cup and gave thanks. This custom deals with the Jewish marriage ceremony. There are books available concerning the significance of these symbols in relation to the Bride of Christ, and therefore, I will not take space here to discuss that area.

The head of the household would, once again, pronounce a universal blessing. The exact prayer in Hebrew was:

> *Baruh Atah Adonai Eloheinu Meleh ha-olam borei p'ri ha-gafen.*

Translated to English, it says:

> *We praise You, O God, King of the Universe, Who creates the fruit of the vine.*

Next Jesus said, *"Drink ye all of it; for this is my blood of the New Testament, which is shed for many for the remission of sins"* (Matthew 26:28). The significance is obvious. Jesus said, *"I am the Vine,"* (John 15:5), but the blessing is not on the vine, nor the branches, but on the fruit of the vine—the Church. In this way, Jesus predicted the birth of the Church, His Bride, and sealed it by partaking of the wine and encouraging His followers to also partake.

In doing this, Jesus was saying, "Fellows, I am soon to die. I will live again, but in a dimension not yet known to man. Now I am only *with* you, but soon I will be *in* you. I am about to birth on this planet a group of people who will walk in an authority that is not of this world. They will live by Kingdom principles and have Kingdom demonstration." He was saying that He would bless His offspring, the fruit of the vine, for greater achievements than ever before.

When the Jews celebrate Passover, they are celebrating thousands of years of freedom from bondage in Egypt. When you and I celebrate Communion, we are celebrating freedom from sin and our hope of eternal life.

To close this chapter, I want to share with you why I believe Communion is so important. What I am about to say is not just my opinion; it is very biblical; and I believe it will

When you and I celebrate Communion, we are celebrating freedom from sin and our hope of eternal life!

bless you, even as it did me, when I began to see it in God's Word.

First, did you ever notice that Communion was the last thing that Jesus and His disciples did together before His death? Therefore, I believe it is appropriate to say that this is a very important act. This importance is illustrated by His words, *"this do in remembrance of me"* (Luke 22:19). Communion is something that believers should look forward to and something they should do and enjoy doing.

My mother passed away very young, but before her departure from this earth, she gave me something very special to keep, a special gift from her to me. It was her hope that this special gift would remind me of her, and it has. Although that gift could never be as valuable to me as was the actual presence of my mother, I cherish it, as you can imagine. No amount of money could buy that gift from me.

In the same way, Jesus told us to participate in Communion *"in remembrance"* of Him. Communion, therefore, should be a constant reminder of what our Lord Jesus did for us and how we are to benefit from His sacrifice. Too often, I fear, when we partake of Communion, our thoughts are elsewhere, not where Jesus intended. He said:

THIS DO IN REMEMBRANCE OF ME

We should each cherish Communion as His special gift to us, a means of maintaining HIM, HIS LOVE AND HIS SACRIFICE FOR US in our memory. Jesus didn't say, "Do miracles in remembrance of Me," "Build great buildings in remembrance of Me, or "Operate in spiritual gifts in remembrance of Me." Instead, He said, "As you partake of Communion, *this do in remembrance of me.*"

From what I can gather, the first encounter Jesus had with any of His disciples after His death and resurrection took place on the road to Emmaus. These disciples didn't recognize Jesus, but when they arrived at their destination, they constrained Him to stay with them and He consented.

When a meal was served, something strange happened:

We should each cherish Communion as His special gift to us, a means of maintaining HIM, HIS LOVE AND HIS SACRIFICE FOR US in our memory!

He took bread, and blessed it, and brake, and gave it to them. And their eyes were opened, and they knew Him. Luke 24:30-31

Jesus' participation with His disciples in Communion was justified. They had been deeply saddened by His death. Now He brought back to them the memory of His prophecy concerning the resurrection, and suddenly *"their eyes were opened."*

I firmly believe that Communion is meant to be an eye-opener for us. There are things that take place in Communion services that happen at no other time.

When this was all over, and the men began to think back on it, traveling all that way with Jesus and not even recognizing that it was Jesus, they said, *"Did not our heart burn within us, while he talked with us by the way, and while he opened to us the scriptures?"* (Luke 24:32). Then, they immediately arose and went back to Jerusalem and joined the other disciples. To them they declared:

Communion: Past and Present

The Lord is risen indeed, and hath appeared to [us].   Luke 24:34

There was no longer any shadow of doubt. When did they know that it was Jesus? When He broke the bread and gave thanks (see Verse 35).

Friend, your countenance would be sad too if your Lord is dead. You would have every right in the world to hang you head and be teary eyed. But partake of His blood and body and allow Jesus to open your eyes, and you will celebrate life as never before.

Finally, Communion will be the first thing Jesus does when He and His Bride are ultimately united at the end of this age at the Marriage Supper of the Lamb. God's Word tells us that it is our Father's good pleasure to give us His Kingdom (see Luke 12:32). Jesus also said:

> *I appoint unto you a kingdom, as my Father hath appointed unto me; that ye may eat and drink at my table in my kingdom.*
>   Luke 22:29-30

I firmly believe that Communion is meant to be an eye-opener for us. There are things that take place in Communion services that happen at no other time!

These words were prophetically spoken prior to the Passover and prior to Jesus' death. Luke also tells us that one day Jesus will gird Himself, make us to sit down to meat, and then come forth and serve us Himself (see Luke 12:37). As you and I live out Kingdom principles, preparing this earth for our Lord's return, He will ultimately be united with His Church. Then, quite appropriately, the first event on the calender will be to serve us Communion. God has set the protocol; we rejoice in the acknowledgement of it and the participation in it.

4

COMMUNION AND COVENANT

And Melchizedek king of Salem brought forth bread and wine: and he was the priest of the most high God. And he blessed him, and said, Blessed be Abram of the most high God, possessor of heaven and earth: and blessed be the most high God, which hath delivered thine enemies into thy hand. And he gave him tithes of all.

And the king of Sodom said unto Abram, Give me the persons, and take the goods to thyself.

And Abram said to the king of Sodom, I have lift up mine hand unto the LORD, the most high God, the possessor of heaven and earth, that I will not take from a thread even to a shoelatchet, and that I will not take any thing that is thine, lest thou shouldest say, I have made Abram rich.   Genesis 14:18-23

For when God made promise to Abraham, because he could swear by no greater, he sware by himself, saying, Surely blessing I will bless thee, and multiplying I will multiply thee.

And so, after he had patiently endured, he obtained the promise. For men verily swear by the greater: and an oath for confirmation is to them an end of all strife. Wherein God, willing more abundantly to shew unto the heirs of promise the immutability of his counsel, confirmed it by an oath: that by two immutable things, in which it was impossible for God to lie, we might have a strong consolation, who have fled for refuge to lay hold upon the hope set before us: which hope we have as an anchor of the soul, both sure and stedfast, and which entereth into that within the veil; whither the forerunner is for

Covenant truth goes far beyond the concept of not being blessed, to entertaining a curse. That is the area you hear little or nothing about!

us entered, even Jesus, made an high priest
for ever after the order of Melchisedec.

Hebrews 6:13-20

You may read or hear messages concerning covenant relationship, but the hoopla that accompanies some of them can often mislead you into believing that you have no responsibility in the matter. Also, too often it is implied that if you don't hold up your end of the covenant, you will not be blessed. That, my friend, is only the half of it.

Covenant truth goes far beyond the concept of not being blessed, to entertaining a curse. That is the area you hear little or nothing about. As you enter into a contractual agreement here on earth (and contracts are common in the secular world), there are definite benefits for upholding your end of the deal, and there are also penalties for not doing so.

Since we are more than aware of the benefits to be derived from covenant with the Lord, I will not deal with those in detail here. In fact, I will also not go into great detail on the penalties either, except perhaps to state the obvious. What I feel compelled to show you is that Communion is a covenant you make with God and that God makes with you.

My prayer is that God will help me to give you His counsel on this subject. One thing is sure: we must move out from the norm and into the supernatural by actually living out our covenant relationship with God. If you are looking for blessings, live out your covenant, and you will not be able to escape the blessings that result.

I believe that the truths I present in this chapter will enhance your life as a believer, and this will enhance your local fellowship. I would go so far as to say that this is one chapter your pastor will truly appreciate. There are some things I say that many shepherds fear to say to their congregations. It is done here to bring healing to your spirit and the assurance of a demonstration of God's provision as we live out Kingdom principles concerning Communion and covenant.

Our text in Genesis describes three areas of covenant relationship that we will discuss.

The Passover was instituted just before the Exodus from Egypt, but could not the God who initiated the Passover allow a "priest of the Most High God" to get in on future events?

There seems to be the implication of complete understanding on the part of the parties involved. The three areas are: Communion, the Priesthood and Tithing.

Abraham was just returning from a victorious conquest when the king of Salem met him. Interestingly enough, Melchizedek, whose order of priesthood was followed by Jesus, came to Abraham with bread and wine. I don't know what that means to you, but to me it means Communion.

The Passover was instituted just before the Exodus from Egypt, but could not the God who initiated the Passover allow a *"priest of the Most High God"* to get in on future events? Amos 3:7 and other many other scriptural passages seem to indicate that as a child of God, we can share His plans. I am persuaded that some people would not know if God was speaking to them, even if He appeared personally.

Hebrews 6 records the fact that God made a promise to Abraham, saying to him, *"Blessing I will bless thee and multiplying I will multiply thee."* So, the divine plan of God is to bless and multiply me regardless of my acceptance or rejection of Him. And God guaranteed, or confirmed, His promises with an oath.

This word *oath* is translated from the Hebrew word *horkus,* which is defined as "sacred bound." It is the affirmation of the confirmation: *"He sware by Himself"* (Hebrews 6:13).

Genesis 15:1-19 records the vision of the furnace and lamp. Genesis 22:15-19 deals with the oath of God, along with the blessing. He swore by Himself. There was no greater person to appeal to, so He pledged His own eternal power to fulfill His promises. This is very important. God pledged His own eternal power to fulfill the eternal past, eternal present and eternal future.

Knowing that it is impossible for God to lie, let us examine what I have come to call the destructive power of God. If God's promise would not have come to pass, He would have ceased to be God. He would not have only ceased to be God; He would never have been God in the first place. If God lied, He would cease to be God. He would self-destruct.

God pledged His own eternal power to fulfill the eternal past, eternal present and eternal future!

If man destroys himself, you still know he was a man. The destructive power of man is present and future. But if God destroys Himself, He was never God, and no knowledge of Him would ever have existed. His destruction would have been both present and past.

Now can you see the impact of the oath of God? The strength of that oath rests in Him being God. And this is all part of Communion, tithing and the priesthood. Take hold of this truth so that you may move on in Kingdom living and demonstration. See and understand the strength of this covenant so that you can move on to deeper things.

Next, in the case of Abraham and Melchisedec, we see the priesthood. Once again, there are many books written concerning the priesthood. I only address it here because it is imperative for you to get a complete understanding of your position in Christ. Know whose you are. When you have that knowledge, Hell itself cannot prevail against you.

Some may feel insignificant in the light of the talents and abilities of others, but I have some good news for you: there are no insignificant people among those who are in covenant with God. In Christ, you are a priest and a king unto the King of Kings and the Lord of Lords.

It is easy for most to accept teachings concerning Communion and the priesthood, but when you mention tithing, it seems that an invisible blanket comes over many. This should not be. Actually, Communion, the priesthood and tithing are inseparable. You cannot have one of them without the others. The priesthood is entered upon at salvation, Communion is your acceptance of the priesthood, and tithing seals your acceptance.

People use many reasons not to tithe, but none of them hold up under close scrutiny. The excuse most often employed is: "I would tithe, but I just can't afford it." If you have used that reasoning, my question to you is this: "Are you really tithing scripturally?"

In Genesis 14:20, the last two words contain God's program for our tithing. Again, it says:

Communion, the priesthood and tithing are inseparable. You cannot have one of them without the others!

Communion and Covenant

And blessed be the most high God, which hath delivered thine enemies into thy hand. And he gave him tithes OF ALL.

"OF ALL." "Well," many say, "I give my tenth." But I wonder if the tenth was used as a maximum or a minimum? In far too many cases, I fear, Christians have used the tenth as a maximum, and the result is that the Kingdom of God has suffered, and the tither has suffered as well.

If we were to ask, "Do you tithe OF ALL?" too many would have to answer, "Oh, no, just what I bring in at home." This shows that they have allowed Satan to slip in through a "theological loophole" (in other words, a lie), and cause them to slip into complacency and negligence and stop fulfilling their ministry as a priest!

The problem here is no longer an issue of percentages; it has become a problem of the spirit. Every man's sincerity is judged by the heart, and God is the Righteous Judge.

Priest of God, you are not your own, and

what you "possess" is not yours either. It has been entrusted to your care by Almighty God for the sake of His Kingdom. If you dare to claim the promises of God, you would do well to recall the covenant: *"all that I have is thine."*

Believer, each time you receive Communion and you do not tithe God's way, you are bringing damnation upon yourself and your home. The devourer takes advantage of your complacency by devastating your family and whatever else is of value to you. He is not rebuked through prayer and fasting; he is rebuked through tithing. Why? Because tithing is part of the covenant.

Malachi 3:10 speaks of *"meat in mine house."* Too many people sit in church and gripe and complain because there is no manifestation of God's power present. They bring their needs to God in prayer, only to go home with those same needs. The finger of I-do-not-accept-the-blame-for-unanswered-prayer; it-must-be-your-fault is pointed at the pastor and the church, and it is the individual believer who suffers.

If you want healing, then tithe (along with everything else God expects of you). If you want prosperity, then tithe. If you want consistency in your walk with God, then tithe!

If you want healing, then tithe (along with everything else God expects of you). If you want prosperity, then tithe. If you want consistency in your walk with God, then tithe. Your needs are wrapped up in that word Malachi spoke—*meat*. If there is no meat in God's house, it is because of a lack of tithers. Become a tither, and Heaven's windows will open to pour out to you more meat than you will be able to contain. You will then have Kingdom demonstration. Souls will be added to the Kingdom, lives will be set at liberty and all nations will call you blessed. Praise God!

God is challenging us these days to live like Kingdom people, and it is your covenant with Communion to tithe as a priest.

5

DISCERNING THE LORD'S BODY

And when he had given thanks, he brake it, and said, Take, eat: this is my body, which is broken for you: this do in remembrance of me. After the same manner also he took the cup, when he had supped, saying, this cup is the new testament in my blood: this do ye, as oft as ye drink it, in remembrance of me. For as often as ye eat this bread, and drink this cup, ye do shew the Lord's death till he come. Wherefore whosoever shall eat this bread, and drink this cup of the Lord, unworthily, shall be guilty of the body and blood of the Lord. But let a man examine himself, and so let him eat of that bread, and drink of that cup.

For he that eateth and drinketh unworthily, eateth and drinketh damnation to himself, not discerning the Lord's body. For this cause many are weak and sickly among you, and many sleep. 1 Corinthians 11:24-30

As we have seen in an earlier chapter, this text, written by Paul to the Corinthian believers, is probably the most misused text in the entire canon of scripture. Opinions are formed, the routine of one is copied, and the Church suffers. In the process, a philosophy of unworthiness is passed on that has glorified the flesh of a few people but made the majority of Christians to feel like a second-rate citizen in God's Kingdom.

As a teenager, I recall my pastor serving communion to the church. He did it with a definite warning against partaking unworthily, and he used this text to justify his stand. His definition of *unworthiness,* like the majority of the clergy, was "having some evil (sin) in your life, such as lying, stealing," or just plain "being bad." Needless to say, the fear generated by this

But Paul's admonishment to them was that they examine themselves, not one another!

man, along with many other clergy, hampered many from receiving the Eucharist, and it also caused many to repent secretly. In one particular instance, it caused a family argument, for one member of the family did not partake of Communion, and this raised the curiosity of the spouse as well as others in the congregation.

Clearly, there were members of the church in Corinth who were partaking unworthily. But Paul's admonishment to them was that they examine themselves, not one another. Then, he went on to say, *"let him eat ... and drink."*

Some proper definitions are in order here to enable us to rightly divide the Word of Truth: The word *unworthily* means "irreverently." *Damnation* means "condemnation to eternal punishment in hell." *Discerning* means "to separate thoroughly."

What is this all about? It is to enable us to give honor to whom honor is due. Not recognizing the benefits of the Communion meal or Jesus' work, represented by the Communion meal, is irreverence. To not discern, or thoroughly separate the Lord's Body, leads to damnation, and this penalty involves weakness, sickness and death. Therefore, eating and drinking damnation to oneself is not because there is sin in one's life but, rather, because of not realizing while you are partaking of Communion that you have the means and opportunity to be free from sin, sickness and the other ill effects of the enemy's attacks on your life.

It is not that eating and drinking causes weakness, sickness and dying among Christians; it is that Christians fail to realize that they are partaking of what can actually release them. By failing to realize that, they remain in their present state of being weak or sick, or they may even die (all effects of damnation). This might be a good place to apply the scriptural truth: *"My people are destroyed for lack of knowledge"* (Hosea 4:6).

If you are a minister who has refused to serve Communion to little ones, teens or others or they refused to partake because of fear you may have generated in their lives, I must ask you: "How many times have you eaten and drunk unworthily yourself?" There must be a proper

Eating and drinking damnation to oneself is not because there is sin in one's life but, rather, because of not realizing while you are partaking of Communion that you have the means and opportunity to be free from sin, sickness and the other ill effects of the enemy's attacks on your life!

discerning of the Lord's body so that the manifest power of God can move through us.

"To thoroughly separate" is the main thought of this chapter. I will do my best to deal with certain issues concerning the Lord's body that will lead us to healing in the Body of Christ. This discussion is by no means conclusive, but it can start you off on the right road to discerning His body.

Paul wrote:

> *For if we would judge ourselves, we should not be judged.*   1 Corinthians 11:31

Let us consider four areas of the Lord's Body:

THE LORD'S BODY AS THE COLLECTIVE CHURCH

We are the Body of Christ. All who have repented and accepted Jesus Christ are part of that Body. We are many individual members, but just one Body. The concepts that we are the "House of God," the "Habitation of God," the "Church of God" are well accepted among believers. Therefore, when we come together collectively, we make up the Lord's Body.

Jesus said:

> *My house shall be called the house of prayer.*
> Matthew 21:13

The habitation of God, or His house, is concerned with prayer. The Church is a house of power. The next verse reveals:

> *And the blind and the lame came to him in the temple; and he healed them.*
> Matthew 21:14

Verse 15 reveals us as a body of praise:

> *And when the chief priests and scribes saw the wonderful things that he did, and the children crying in the temple, and saying, Hosanna to the son of David; they were sore displeased.*

We are the Body of Christ. All who have repented and accepted Jesus Christ are part of that Body!

The Scriptures teach us that God inhabits the praises of His people:

> *But thou art holy, O thou that inhabitest the praises of Israel.* Psalm 22:3

These are the fruits of the collective Body of Christ. The important question here is: "How do I fail to discern that?" The answer is: by neglecting or refusing to come together as a house of prayer, power and praise.

Friend, you cannot make it on you own in this life. You are not an island to yourself. An elder minister reminded me years ago that a single banana can easily be plucked and peeled. If you are alone in you endeavor for the Lord, you may get skinned. If you choose to sever yourself from the Body of the Lord, you position yourself for damnation.

Hebrews 10:25 has a few interesting details that may help those who feel they do not need the local church:

Discerning the Lord's Body

Not forsaking the assembling of ourselves together, as the manner of some is; but exhorting one another: and so much the more, as ye see the day approaching.

First of all, I see here a caution being issued: *"not forsaking the assembling of ourselves together."* Who is issuing this caution? It is God Himself who is saying this, not some money-hungry preacher. And why would God exhort us not to forsake the assembling of ourselves together? Because He knows the importance of the various parts of His Body working together.

In the real world, a caution light comes on just before a red light. The caution light means that if you pass the next light that is coming, you will be in trouble. You could even die as a result.

In these days, the enemy has launched an all-out attack against the ministry. His purpose is to stop you from fellowshipping with one another and being part of the entire Body. Satan realizes the potential of a group of people who come together to worship and serve God. This is what will ultimately destroy his kingdom. Therefore, even in the midst of adversity, never stop coming together.

Next, I see in Hebrews 10:25 a criticism: *"as the manner of some is."* Believe me, God is not commending the actions of these independent-minded people; He is criticizing them. I can only imagine the thoughts of God concerning those who somehow believe they do not need others in the Kingdom of God. How could they sustain each other?

God's Word is clear on this point:

> *And the eye cannot say unto the hand, I have no need of thee: nor again the head to the feet, I have no need of you.* 1 Corinthians 12:21

Oh, my friend, beware of the one who thinks he can make it on his own. He is on a path to self-destruction and is trying to bring you down with him. Heed the caution sign and hear God's criticism of this dangerous attitude.

Third, I see in Hebrews 10:25 a commission: *"but exhorting one another."* What does

Beware of the one who thinks he can make it on his own. He is on a path to self-destruction and is trying to bring you down with him!

exhort mean? It means to encourage, deliver, strengthen, comfort, entreat and pray for one another. We will have trouble doing all of that if we fail to discern the Lord's Body.

Fourth, I see in Hebrews 10:25 a charge: *"and so much the more."* Neighbor, this is not the time to throw in the towel. It is not the time to stop supporting the ministry. This is the time to take charge of the situation. This is not the time for withholding your support of the Church; it is time for doubling up our efforts in the work of the Lord. This is not a time to quit; it is time to press in and press on.

Finally, I see in Hebrews 10:25 a consistency: *"as ye see the day approaching."* The end of this age is approaching, and as we see that fact, we must become consistent with our witness.

Much more could be said concerning the Lord's Body represented by the Church, but I believe these few facts will enlighten you to search for deeper things concerning His Body.

THE LORD'S BODY AS INDIVIDUALS IN THE KINGDOM

Although united together we make up the Lord's Body, we are still individuals within that Body. The thought I want to share with you concerning this area deals with the proper regard we are to have for one another. I feel that my personal experience is adequate in dealing with this area.

I was the second child of ten born to Wesley and Daisy Fitch. We were somewhat poor and were considered, at the time, to be "low class." My parents, being a proud set, did their best to cover up this "classification."

I was raised most of my life on a sugar cane plantation in a small town in Louisiana, and I slept, ate and drank (H_2O) with the black laborers. Neither my pigment nor theirs rubbed off on the other, but I rarely had any trouble with them. I did have trouble with some of the the white laborers.

Daddy was a hard-working man, and he provided for us the best way he knew how. Mama

This is not a time to quit; it is
time to press in and press on!

taught us manners and exerted every bit of her four-foot-ten-inch frame in disciplinary actions and in making us into a family.

For over a year, a lady named Sister Shirley would visit our humble home every evening and invite us to attend church with her. But we were good Catholics (meaning that we attended church twice a year—Easter and Christmas) and, therefore, felt that we did not need any more church. Still, God gave that lady a vision of our entire family saved and serving God.

Finally, after a year of Sister Shirley's visits and her much talking, my parents consented to go to church with her. They came back home that day and told us that they had gotten "saved." This was new terminology for us, and we wondered what it could mean. They made us all go to that church, and we all got saved.

Someday I would love to write an autobiography, for our story is quite interesting. But, for now, I must get on with the text. I said all that to say this: the world of my youth not only referred to us as "low class"; the church did the same thing. It seems that all we were to that church were numbers on a board, some additional funds coming into the church coffers (Daddy was a very liberal giver) and someone who was available to do the dirty work of the church that no one else was willing to do. Had not my experience with God been genuine, I would have turned my back on Him, that church and the whole works and never serve Him again. Today I rejoice in God that He is faithful in keeping what He has saved.

Every time Communion was served in the church, I, like the others, partook of it. I did it with the sincere faith that God could make my life better. And, praise God, He did. He changed me and my surroundings.

At a very young age, I began to see my potential in God, and today I am still working to fulfill His good pleasure in my life.

The Scriptures teach us:

> *Be kindly affectioned one to another with brotherly love; in honour preferring one another.* Romans 12:10

I partook of Communion with the sincere faith that God could make my life better. And, praise God, He did!

Let nothing be done through strife or vain-glory; but in lowliness of mind let each esteem other better than themselves.

Philippians 2:3

To discern the Body of the Lord means to have proper regard one for another. To the people we consider as not very important in the Kingdom, God says that He bestows *"more abundant honour"* (1 Corinthians 12:23).

It is because of His hedge around me today that I can write and help you see the importance of each individual in His glorious Kingdom. Not discerning the Lord's Body in this area brings damnation to an individual.

One of the reasons many churches do not believe in or practice healing is that they have not discerned the Lord's Body among their members. They have racial differences and do not regard each other as they should. May we stop excusing our lack of productivity in the Kingdom of God, address the problem and appropriate the solution so that healing can come to the Body.

Religions, denominations and certain individuals have dealt me many a hard blow, but I can say, like Polycarp of old, "He has done me nothing but good."

THE LORD'S BODY AS THE SACRAMENT

We must have an understanding of the significance of the blood and the body of our Lord Jesus Christ. This was dealt with in chapter 2, but here I would like to insert a couple of thoughts that may provoke you to search a little deeper. 1 John 2:1-2 tells us that Jesus is the propitiation for our sins:

> *My little children, these things write I unto you, that ye sin not. And if any man sin, we have an advocate with the Father, Jesus Christ the righteous: and he is the propitiation for our sins: and not for ours only, but also for the sins of the whole world.*

We must have an understanding
of the significance of the blood and
the body of our Lord Jesus Christ!

Discerning the Lord's Body

We know that Jesus is our substitute, our atonement, but the deeper sense of that scripture is that He is the One who turns away all wrath for us. I will leave it at that and allow you to study it more in detail for yourself.

Also, I submit for your observation that before the children of Israel left Egypt, they spoiled the Egyptians. Could it be that God is trying to communicate to us a truth through Communion concerning spoiling the enemy?

The final thought for your consideration is concerning the needed unity of the Body. Jesus prayed:

> *That they all may be one; as thou, Father, art in me, and I in thee, that they also may be one in us: that the world may believe that thou hast sent me.*　　John 17:21

When you think about it, that was an amazingly powerful prayer. We are to be one to the same degree that Jesus was one with the Father in Heaven. Think about that!

And finally, consider the power found in partaking of His flesh and the drinking of His blood:

Then Jesus said unto them, Verily, verily, I say unto you, Except ye eat the flesh of the Son of man, and drink his blood, ye have no life in you. Whoso eateth my flesh, and drinketh my blood, hath eternal life; and I will raise him up at the last day. For my flesh is meat indeed, and my blood is drink indeed. He that eateth my flesh, and drinketh my blood, dwelleth in me, and I in him. As the living Father hath sent me, and I live by the Father: so he that eateth me, even he shall live by me.   John 6:53-57

Wow! There is so much more for all of us.

DISCERNING THE LORD'S BODY IN REFERENCE TO MINISTERIAL AUTHORITY

God has a structure, and no amount of ideas, committees or thinking that we have a better way will change His plan of operation. There

We are to be one to the same degree that Jesus was one with the Father in Heaven. Think about that!

are far too many insurrections in His Body as it is. It seems as though many Christians do not adhere to the Word concerning authority. For this cause, many are weak, sick and already sleep. Friend, if you reject God's man, you are rejecting God. There is no getting around it; God has set in the Church ministry gifts for the perfecting of the saints, for the work of the ministry and for the edifying of the Body. The end result of ignoring this is opening yourself up for the ill effects of a crime. You cannot even begin to reach perfection and maturity if you reject Kingdom authority.

Some insist, "I don't need some man to teach me; I have the Holy Ghost." I seriously doubt that they do if they reject God's authority. If these so-called "spiritual" people really do have something, and they do not need any one to lead them, then why are they trying to convince you to follow them? Why don't they give you what they profess to have so you don't have to follow anyone either—especially them?

God will not go against His Word, and neither will He deny Himself. So it is either God who is wrong or that super-spiritual person who is trying to deceive you. I call on you to take heed to the authority that God has given you so you can be healed and brought to maturity in His Kingdom.

There is a place for each of us in that Kingdom, but all too often we try to fill a place that God has not called us to. He said:

> *Are all apostles? are all prophets? are all teachers? are all workers of miracles? Have all the gifts of healing? do all speak with tongues? do all interpret?* 1 Corinthians 12:29-30

The obvious answer is No! Find your place in Christian service and function faithfully there until God says differently. Total satisfaction may not be for you to sing or preach, and if you try to do so, you will know it, and so will everyone else. Do what God has called you to do, for no one can do that better. Then and only then will you realize total satisfaction in your calling.

Recognizing your pastor and other leaders will generate health and healing to the whole Body:

Friend, if you reject God's man, you are rejecting God!

I call on you to take heed to the authority that God has given you so you can be healed and brought to maturity in His Kingdom!

Discerning the Lord's Body

Render therefore to all their dues: tribute to whom tribute is due; custom to whom custom; fear to whom fear; honour to whom honour.   Romans 13:7

Let the elders that rule will be counted worthy of double honor, especially those who labor in the Word and doctrine.
                                    1 Timothy 5:17

I sense a restoration that is coming to the Body of the Lord and, with it, subsequent healing. It will not be because of one man's ability or knowledge, but because the Church as a whole is awakening to the truths of God's Word.

Communion and its reception is only one of the truths that will begin to bridge together that which has been separated and cause a unity to form that will bring the greatest harvest of souls this world has ever known. Reap from the contents of this book the truths of God's Kingdom that He has revealed to me, and then be blessed as you share them with others.

AUTHOR CONTACT PAGE

On the Web:
http://jerryfitchministries.com/

E-mail:
decajun2@aol.com

Phone:
(337) 831-0536

Mail:
Jerry and Monique Fitch
4204 Eldridge Street
New Iberia, LA 70563

BOOKS BY JERRY FITCH

Seasons of Suddenlies

...and other revelations of God's times and seasons

by Dr. Jerry Fitch

Introduction by Dr. Jerry Edmon

Moving through a Season of Grief

You have turned my mourning into joyful dancing.
You have taken away my clothes of mourning and clothed me with joy.
Psalm 30:11

Jerry Fitch

THE

FINAL
CALL

ARE WE PRESENTLY
RECEIVING THE FINAL CALL
OF THE SPIRIT?

JERRY FITCH

COMMUNION

TRUTH
VS.
TRADITION

JERRY FITCH

www.ingramcontent.com/pod-product-compliance
Lightning Source LLC
Chambersburg PA
CBHW051837040426
42447CB00006B/574